A Grandparent's Gift Of Memories

A Pilgrimage With The Saints

Nancy Groves

A Grandparent's Gift of Memories by Nancy Groves
Copyright © 2014 by Nancy Groves

Cover photo: Patron Saints of Grandparents—Saints Anne and Joachim with Mary © zatletic

A Grandparent's Gift of Memories

Contact at:

email address: nangroves@yahoo.com

ISBN – 13: 978-1500845308
ISBN – 10: 1500845302

Printed in the United States of America

First Edition

Dedicated to Ruth Walsh,
my dearest sister, whose love and support
sustain and uplift me on my journey in life.

CHAPTERS OF MY LIFE

PRAYER FOR GRANDPARENTS

Lord Jesus
you were born of the Virgin Mary,
the daughter of Saints Joachim and Anne.
Look with love on grandparents the world over.
Protect them! They are a source of enrichment
for families, for the Church and for all of society.
Support them! As they grow older,
may they continue to be for their families
strong pillars of Gospel faith,
guardians of noble domestic ideals,
living treasuries of sound religious traditions.
Make them teachers of wisdom and courage,
that they may pass on to future generations the fruits
of their mature human and spiritual experience.

Lord Jesus,
help families and society
to value the presence and role of grandparents.
May they never be ignored or excluded,
but always encounter respect and love.
Help them to live serenely and to feel welcomed
in all the years of life which you give them.
Mary, Mother of all the living,
keep grandparents constantly in your care,
accompany them on their earthly pilgrimage,
and by your prayers, grant that all families
may one day be reunited in our heavenly homeland,
where you await all humanity
for the great embrace of life without end. Amen!

Benedictus II pp

"Children and the elderly build the future of peoples: children because they lead history forward, the elderly because they transmit the experience and wisdom of their lives."

"How precious is the family as the privileged place for transmitting the faith. How important grandparents are for family life, for passing on the human and religious heritage which is so essential for each and every society!"

Pope Francis

Introduction

God touches every life. In telling my story,
I will praise Him.

I am blessed with the privilege of being your grandparent. This is my life story. I share it in hopes of imparting to you a quiet truth—that throughout my life—through milestones celebrated, joys shared, heartaches experienced, obstacles faced—there was always—surrounding me and lifting me up—the amazing grace and love of God. May my life story be a humble testament to you of the faith that sustains me and may we celebrate that faith together.

"If we would completely rejoice the heart of God, let us strive in all things to conform ourselves to his divine will."

Saint Alphonsus Liguori

I pray that the God of our Lord Jesus Christ, the Father of glory, may give you a spirit of wisdom and revelation as you come to know him, so that, with the eyes of your heart enlightened, you may know what is the hope to which he has called you, what are the riches of his glorious inheritance among the saints, and what is the immeasurable greatness of his power for us who believe . . .

Ephesians 1:17-19

BEGINNINGS

St. Gerard Majella

Patron Saint of Expectant Mothers

Birth: 1725 Death: 1755

Canonized: 1904

Feast Day: October 16

St. Gerard Majella felt called to Monastic life when he was 23. In 1752, he joined the Redemptorists and became a lay brother. While there, he served as gardener, porter, and tailor. In spite of these humble tasks, he exhibited great devotion and spent hours in prayer. His time spent with the Redemptorists revealed his gifts of clairvoyance, mystic knowledge, and miraculous healings. During his life, he performed many wonders. He became known for his great humility, generosity, and profound wisdom. In his words, "Who except God can give you peace? Has the world ever been able to satisfy the heart?"

For it was you who formed my inward parts; you knit me together in my mother's womb. I praise you, for I am fearfully and wonderfully made . . . On you I was cast from my birth, and since my mother bore me you have been my God.

Psalm: 139:13; 22:10

Reflections

Where were you born?

In what city or town was your first home? What do you re-member about that home?

What was popular and newsworthy on the day of your birth? (headlines, songs, movies, books, TV shows, fashions)

What are some amusing stories from your years as a toddler?

What are some of your earliest memories of your parents?

When and where were you baptized?

Who are your godparents? How did your godparents encourage the development of your faith through the years?

Did you have a favorite story about Jesus?

CHILDHOOD

St. Nicholas of Myra

Patron Saint of Children

Birth: Middle 3rd century
Death: 4th century

Feast Day: December 6

St. Nicholas was born into a Christian home with loving and devout parents. After being orphaned as a young man, he dedicated his life to helping widows, children, and the poor. Stories are told of his kindness in providing dowries for three young girls and saving three unjustly condemned men from death. In the 4th century, he became the Bishop of Myra. He strongly supported the Christian faith and worked vigorously against paganism. He is known for the depth of his faith, his generosity, and love of children.

But Jesus called for them and said, 'Let the little children come to me, and do not stop them; for it is to such as these that the kingdom of God belongs.'

Luke 18:16

Reflections

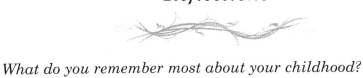

What do you remember most about your childhood?

What are your fondest memories of your mother?

What are your fondest memories of your father?

What did you enjoy most about your siblings?

What childhood memories bring a smile to your face?

How did you celebrate birthdays?

What pets did you have growing up?

What elementary school did you attend? What did you like best about school?

_____

_____

_____

_____

_____

_____

_____

_____

_____

_____

What did you want to be when you grew up?

_____

_____

_____

_____

_____

_____

_____

_____

_____

_____

_____

_____

How old were you when you made your First Communion? What are your memories of that day and how do you remember feeling?

What religious activities do you remember sharing with your parents?

YOUTH

St. Aloysius Gonzaga

Patron Saint of Youth

Birth: 1568 Death: 1591

Canonized: 1726

Feast Day: June 21

St. Aloysius Gonzaga spent his early life surrounded by royalty as his mother was lady-in-waiting to the Queen of Spain and his father was the Marquis of Castiglione. His parents expected him to have an impressive military career. However, Aloysius was a pious youth and was drawn to a devout Christian path. At 17, he entered the Jesuit order. He died at 23, having contracted the plague while caring for the ill at the Jesuits' hospital. In his words, "It is better to be a child of God than king of the whole world."

Shun your youthful passions and pursue righteousness, faith, love, and peace, along with those who call on the Lord from a pure heart.

2 Timothy 2:22

YOUTH

St. Maria Goretti

Patron Saint of Youth

Birth: 1890 Death: 1902

Canonized: 1950

Feast Day: July 6

When Maria was 11 years old, she was abducted from her home by a neighbor, Alessandro. She resisted his attempts to assault her and was stabbed several times. Although mortally wounded, she forgave Alessandro before she died. Alessandro spent 30 years in prison. After 8 years, he repented and upon his release, he asked Maria's mother for forgiveness. In response, she offered him mercy and forgave him. St. Maria is a model for chastity, love, and forgiveness.

Let no one despise your youth, but set the believers an example in speech and conduct, in love, in faith, in purity.

1 Timothy 4:12

Reflections

What are your favorite memories of your youth?

How would you describe yourself during your youth and teen years?

What did you enjoy most about being a teenager?

What was difficult in your teen years?

What were some of your favorite things? (music, books, etc.)

What junior high and high school did you attend? What were your best subjects?

What extracurricular activities did you participate in?

What were some highlights from your school years?

Who was your favorite teacher (teachers) and why?

Who or what was most important in guiding your teenage years?

How did your parents share their faith with you?

When and where were you confirmed? What do you remember about that day?

Did you notice any change in you or your practice of faith after receiving The Sacrament of Confirmation? If so, what were the changes?

Who or what was most important in guiding your spiritual development?

How did your faith influence your teen years?

Education & Vocation

St. Thomas Aquinas

Patron Saint of Learning

Birth: 1225 Death: 1274

Canonized: 1323

Feast Day: January 28

St. Thomas Aquinas was a Dominican friar and an outstanding theologian. During his childhood, he was in the care of the Benedictines of Monte Casino. At the age of 17, he joined the Dominicans of Naples and went on to study at Cologne under St. Albert the Great. When he was 22, he began teaching and publishing his works, and at 26, received his doctorate in Paris. His deep devotion to God was exemplified in his daily life and in his philosophical, scriptural, and theological writings. Many regard him as one of the great theologians of the Middle Ages. In his words, "We are like children, who stand in need of masters to enlighten us and direct us; and God has provided for this, by appointing his angels to be our teachers and guides."

Without eyes there is no light; without knowledge there is no wisdom.

Sirach 3:25

For this very reason, you must make every effort to support your good faith with goodness, and goodness with knowledge . . .

2 Peter 1:5

Education & Vocation

St. Alphonsus Liguori

Patron Saint of Vocations

Birth: 1696 Death: 1787

Canonized: 1839

Feast Day: August 1

St. Alphonsus Liguori was born into Neapolitan nobility. He entered law school at an early age and gained great success in this occupation. After losing an important case, and with much intro-spection, he left his legal career and began his conversion to religious life. After his theological studies, he was ordained priest at the age of 30. Six years later (1732), he founded the Congregation of the Holy Redeemer (Redemptorists) for priests who were dedicated to serving the poor in the countryside of Naples. He published 36 theological works, with the Moral Theology being his most important endeavor. St. Alphonsus was known for his simple, gentle, and clear style of preaching. Encouraging devotion, he wrote Visits to the Most Blessed Sacrament and the Blessed Virgin Mary, containing his reflections and meditations for each of his 31 visits. In 1762, at the age of 66, he was appointed Bishop of Sant'Agatha dei Goti. In his words, "He who trusts himself is lost. He who trusts God can do all things."

. . . lead a life worthy of the calling to which you have been called, with all humility, and gentleness, with patience, bearing with one another in love, making every effort to maintain the unity of the Spirit in the bond of peace.

Ephesians: 4:1-3

Reflections

What were your goals after high school? Did you consider this your vocation?

What type of continued higher education did you pursue?

What were some highlights as you worked toward your vocation?

Did your vocation and life path turn out as you expected?

What did you like most about your chosen vocation?

What advice would you give in seeking the path God has for you?

Marriage

St. Valentine of Rome

Patron Saint of Lovers

Lived and died in the 3rd century

Feast Day: February 14

St. Valentine was a priest in Rome who aided Christians being persecuted under Emperor Claudius II. Refusing to renounce his faith, he was imprisoned where he remained devout and humble in spite of the ordeals he faced. While in prison, he restored the sight to his jailer's blind daughter. St. Valentine's life was one of courage and compassion.

Above all, clothe yourselves with love, which binds everything together in perfect harmony. And let the peace of Christ rule in your hearts to which indeed you were called in the one body. And be thankful.

Colossians 3:14-15

Love is patient; love is kind; love is not envious or boastful or arrogant or rude. It does not insist on its own way; it is not irritable or resentful; it does not rejoice in wrongdoing, but rejoices in the truth. It bears all things, believes all things, hopes all things, endures all things.

1 Corinthians 13:4-7

Marriage

St. Rita of Cascia

Patron Saint of Matrimonial
Difficulties

Birth: 1377 Death: 1447

Canonized: 1900

Feast Day: May 22

St. Rita's childhood wish was to become a nun. However, her parents insisted that she marry, and she deferred to their wishes. For 18 years, she was wed to a cruel, unfaithful, and violent man. Her release from this difficult and unhappy life came with her husband's death. She then pursued her desire to become a nun and tried to join the Augustinian convent in Cascia, where she was denied because she was not a virgin. In 1407, however, the order reconsidered her request and allowed her to enter. While there, she spent many hours in prayer and devoted herself to the care of the sick and counseling sinners. During the final 15 years of her life, she carried a wound on her forehead that resembled the crown of thorns. She was revered for her devotion and her beneficence. After her death, there were many accounts of miracles at Cascia.

Bear with one another and, if anyone has a complaint against another, forgive each other; just as the Lord has forgiven you, so you also must forgive.

Colossians 3:13

Reflections

When did you first meet your husband/wife?

What were the circumstances?

What qualities attracted you to him / her?

When and where were you married?

What memories do you have of your wedding day?

Where did you go on your honeymoon?

Where was your first home? Describe it.

How did you celebrate your faith in your marriage?

What were some difficulties you faced together?

How did your faith help you during those difficult times?

What do you love most about your husband/wife now?

FAMILY

THE HOLY FAMILY
Feast Day: First Sunday after Christmas

MARY, QUEEN OF HEAVEN AND EARTH
Feast Day: August 22

ST. JOSEPH
Feast Day: March 19

CHRIST THE KING
Feast Day: Last liturgical Sunday of the year

Now after they had left, an angel of the Lord appeared to Joseph in a dream and said, 'Get up, take the child and his mother, and flee to Egypt, and remain there until I tell you,' . . . Then Joseph got up, took the child and his mother by night, and went to Egypt and remained there until the death of Herod.

Matthew 2:13-14

For this reason I bow my knees before the Father, from whom every family in heaven and on earth takes its name.

Ephesians 3: 14-15

Reflections

What are the names and birth dates of your children? Were any of your children named after someone in your family?

What is your favorite memory of each child?

What did you love most about each child?

What was the most rewarding aspect of being a parent?

What was the most challenging aspect of being a parent?

What family vacations, trips, activities do you especially remember?

What were some of your family traditions?

What religious traditions did your family follow?

How did you celebrate the holidays?

How did you weave your faith into the fabric of family life?

What legacy would you like to leave your family?

FRIENDSHIPS

St. John—the Apostle

Patron Saint of Friendship

Birth: c 6 Death: c 104

Feast Day: December 27

St. John and his brother James were fishermen in Galilee before being called by Jesus to be his disciples. John is known as the "beloved disciple," affirming the closeness he shared with Jesus. He was present at Jesus' transfiguration and the agony at Gethsemane. At the crucifixion, Jesus entrusted the care of his mother to John. The Divinity of Christ and the importance of love shared between God and his Son and Jesus and his disciples were the focus of John's writings in the fourth gospel. In his later years, John founded many churches in Asia Minor.

A friend loves at all times . . .

Proverbs 17:17

This is my commandment, that you love one another as I have loved you. No one has greater love than this, to lay down one's life for one's friends.

John 15: 12-13

Reflections

Who were your best friends in your childhood and teenage years?

What drew you to them?

What friendships have remained through the years and what friendships are new?

How have your friendships changed through the years?

What qualities do you value most in a friend?

What memories do you have of your most cherished friends?

How has your faith directed you in cultivating friendships and in being a good friend?

Joys & Challenges

St. Philip Neri

Patron Saint of Joy

Birth: 1515 Death: 1595

Canonized: 1622

Feast Day: May 26

St. Philip Neri was a priest in Rome whose lighthearted and friendly manner drew many people to hear his teachings of God. Through his example, he taught humility, tolerance, and service to others. He founded the Congregation of the Oratory where he received the poor and deeply troubled. In his words, "Cheerfulness strengthens the heart and makes us persevere in a good life. Therefore, the servant of God ought always to be in good spirits."

You show me the path of life. In your presence there is fullness of joy . . .

Psalm 16:11

Joys & Challenges

Our Lady of Perpetual Help

Feast Day: June 27

Our Lady of Perpetual Help is a Byzantine icon from the 13th century. The Mother of God is presented holding the child Jesus who finds comfort in her arms. The Archangels Michael and Gabriel hold the images of His Passion. Jesus clasps the right hand of Mary, assured of his safety while in her presence. Our Lady's expression conveys majesty, sorrow, and compassion.

Then will I go to the altar of God, to God my exceeding joy; and I will praise you with the harp, O God, my God. Why are you cast down, O my soul, and why are you disquieted within me? Hope in God; for I shall again praise him, my help and my God.

Psalm 43: 4-5

Reflections

What were the happiest times in your life?

What joyful expectations do you have for the future?

What are you most proud of?

What do you like most about yourself?

What challenges have you faced in your life?

What helped you to overcome them? What role did your faith play? How did the hand of God assist you as you faced these challenges?

What did you learn about your relationship with God as you faced these difficult times?

BELIEFS & VIRTUES

CHRIST THE KING

Feast Day: Last liturgical
Sunday of the year

'Do not let your hearts be troubled. Believe in God, believe also in me.'

John 14:1

Jesus said to him, 'I am the way, and the truth, and the life. No one comes to the Father except through me.'

John 14:6

So we have known and believe the love that God has for us. God is love, and those who abide in love abide in God, and God abides in them.

1John 4:16

Jesus said to her, 'I am the resurrection and the life. Those who believe in me, even though they die, will live.'

John 11:25

Finally, beloved, whatever is true, whatever is honourable, whatever is just, whatever is pure, whatever is pleasing, whatever is commendable, if there is any excellence and if there is anything worthy of praise, think about these things.

Philippians 4:8

Reflections

What virtues in your Catholic faith do you hold dear to your heart?

What virtues do you hope your children learned from you?

How do your Catholic beliefs and your relationships with God's saints leave their mark on your life?

After which saint or saints would you like to model your life? Why?

What are your favorite scriptures and prayers? Which ones are remembered during the good times and the more difficult times?

On Becoming a Grandparent

St. Anne & St. Joachim

Mother and Father of the Blessed Virgin Mary

Patron Saints of Grandparents

Feast Day: July 26

After 20 years of a childless marriage, an angel appeared to Anne and Joachim with news that their desire to have a child would be fulfilled. The child of whom the angel spoke was Mary, beloved Mother of Jesus. After their daughter's birth, St. Anne and St. Joachim dedicated Mary to God at the temple of Jerusalem. Anne and Joachim became the loving grandparents of Jesus, creating an eternal spiritual heritage for grandparents everywhere.

Grandchildren are the crown of the aged, and the glory of children is their parents.

Proverbs 17:6

Reflections

BEGINNING JOURNEYS IN FAITH

Train children in the right way, and when old, they will not stray.

Proverbs 22:6

How did you bring your faith into the early experiences with your grandchild?

_____

_____

_____

_____

_____

_____

_____

_____

_____

_____

_____

_____

_____

What Bible stories and Catholic children's books did you read to your grandchild?

Which ones were your grandchild's favorites?

Were there any special songs or prayers that your grandchild especially loved?

Reflections

Honoring Parents

Hear, my child, your father's instruction, and do not reject your mother's teaching; for they are a fair garland for your head and pendants for your neck.

Proverbs 1:8

How do you demonstrate your love and respect for the parents of your grandchild?

How do you see your role of grandparent within your grand-child's family life?

What are the blessings that come with this unique role?

Reflections

GROWING IN FAITH

By contrast, the fruit of the Spirit is love, joy, peace, patience, kindness, generosity, faithfulness, gentleness, and self-control . . . If we live by the Spirit, let us also be guided by the Spirit.

Galatians 5:22-23, 25

What are your memories of your grandchild's First Communion? What thoughts did you share with your grandchild at that time?

What memories do you have of your grandchild's confirmation?

How did you support and celebrate your grandchild as he/she received these Sacraments?

How do you manifest and model for your grandchild the "fruit of the Spirit" in your daily life?

Reflections

Gratitude

And let the peace of Christ rule in your hearts, to which indeed you were called in the one body. And be thankful.

Colossians 3:15

When you spend time with your grandchild, for what are you most grateful?

Reflections

LIVING THE CHRISTIAN LIFE

And we urge you, beloved, to admonish the idlers, encourage the faint-hearted, help the weak, be patient with all of them . . . always seek to do good to one another and to all.
1Thessolonians 5:14-15

What events in your life thus far reveal the depth of your faith?

What is the greatest gift of faith you hope to pass on to your grandchild?

REFERENCES

Catholic Church. *Catechism of the Catholic Church*. New York: Doubleday, 1995.

Farmer, David Hugh. *The Oxford Dictionary of Saints, 4th Edition*. Oxford: Oxford University Press, 1997.

Hallam, Elizabeth. *Saints—Who they are and how they help you*. New York: Simon & Schuster, 1994.

Noble, Philip D. *The Watkins Dictionary of Saints*. London: Watkins Publishing, 2007.

Pope Benedict XVI. "Prayer for Grandparents" © Libreria Editrice Vaticana.

Pope Francis. "Angelus, 26 July 2013, Rio de Janeiro." Vatican Website. Libreria Editrice Vaticana, 26 July 2013. Web. 27 Aug. 2014.<http://w2.vatican.va/content/Francesco/en/angelus/2013/documents/papafrancesco_angelus_20130726_gmg-rio.html>

The Scripture quotations contained herein are from the New Revised Standard Version Bible, Catholic Edition, copyright 1989, Division of Christian Education of the National Council of Churches of Christ in the USA. Used with permission. All rights reserved.

ILLUSTRATION CREDITS

Saint Gerard Majella, Creative Commons CCO.10 Universal Public Domain Dedication Wikimedia; Saint Nicholas of Myra, © lindom—canstockphoto.com; Saint Aloysius Gonzaga © zatletic—fotolia.com; Saint Maria Goretti © zatletic—fotolia.com; Saint Thomas Aquinas, © c.crivelli—restoredtradi-

Reflections & Notes

Made in the USA
Columbia, SC
25 October 2018